The Frog

This book has been reviewed
for accuracy by

Jeffrey Briggs, Ph.D.
Professor of Biology
University of Wisconsin—Waukesha

Library of Congress Number: 78-21240

1 2 3 4 5 6 7 8 9 0 83 82 81 80 79

Printed in the United States of America.

Library of Congress Cataloging in Publication Data

Hogan, Paula Z
  The frog.

  Cover title: The life cycle of the frog.
  SUMMARY: Explains in simple terms the life
cycle of the frog.
  1. Frogs — Juvenile literature. [1. Frogs]
I. Strigenz, Geri K. II. Title. III. Title:
The life cycle of the frog.
QL668.E2H72 597'.8   78-21240
ISBN 0-8172-1253-1 lib. bdg.

The
FROG

By Paula Z. Hogan
Illustrations by Geri K. Strigenz

RAINTREE CHILDRENS BOOKS
Milwaukee • Toronto • Melbourne • London

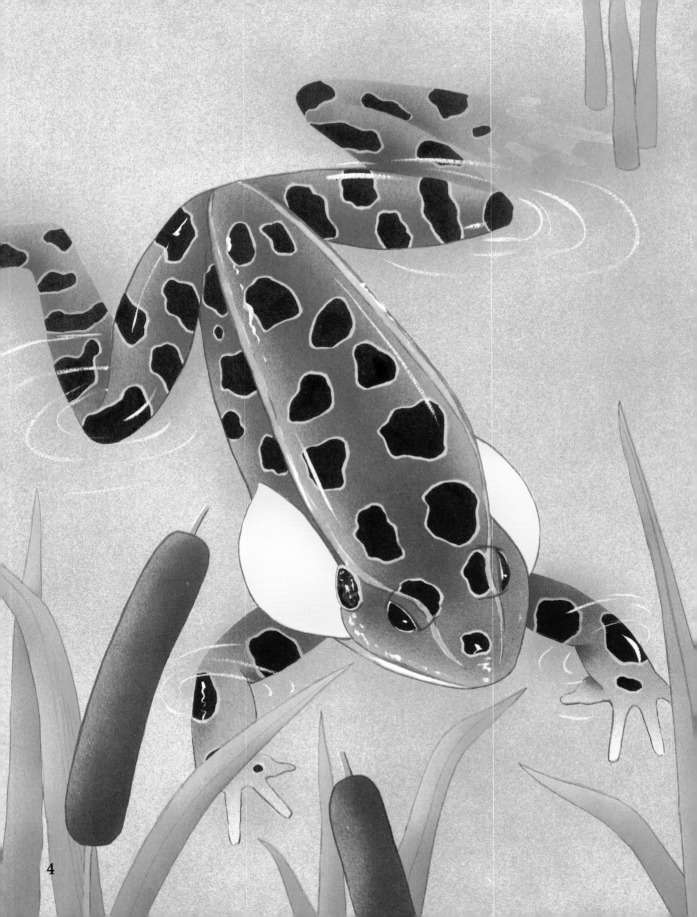

The Frog

It is a cool, spring night. The pond is full of leopard frogs. The male frog croaks. He is calling the female.

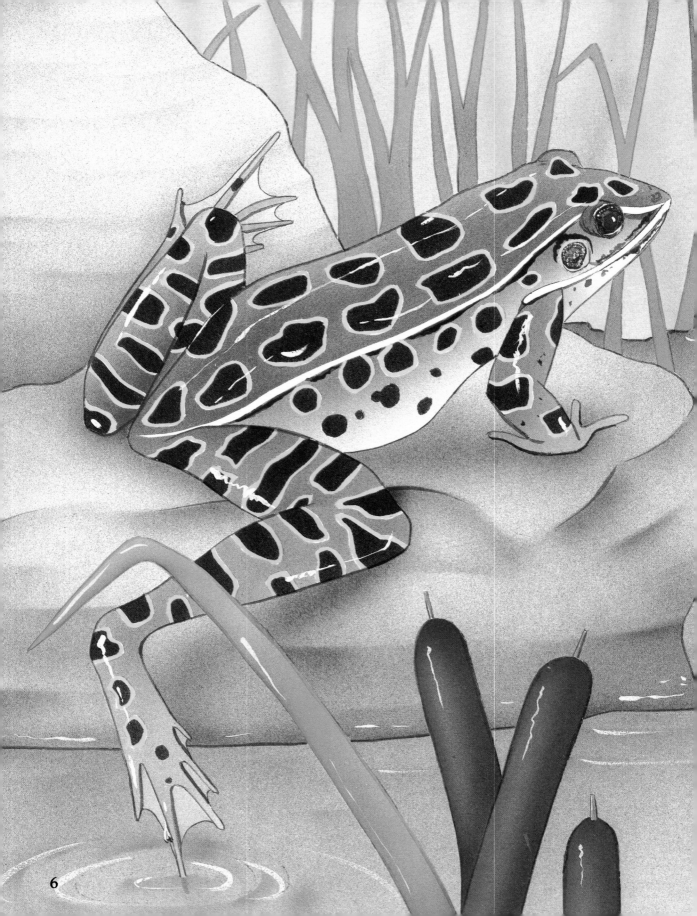

Quietly, the female frog comes near. The male holds her with his front legs.

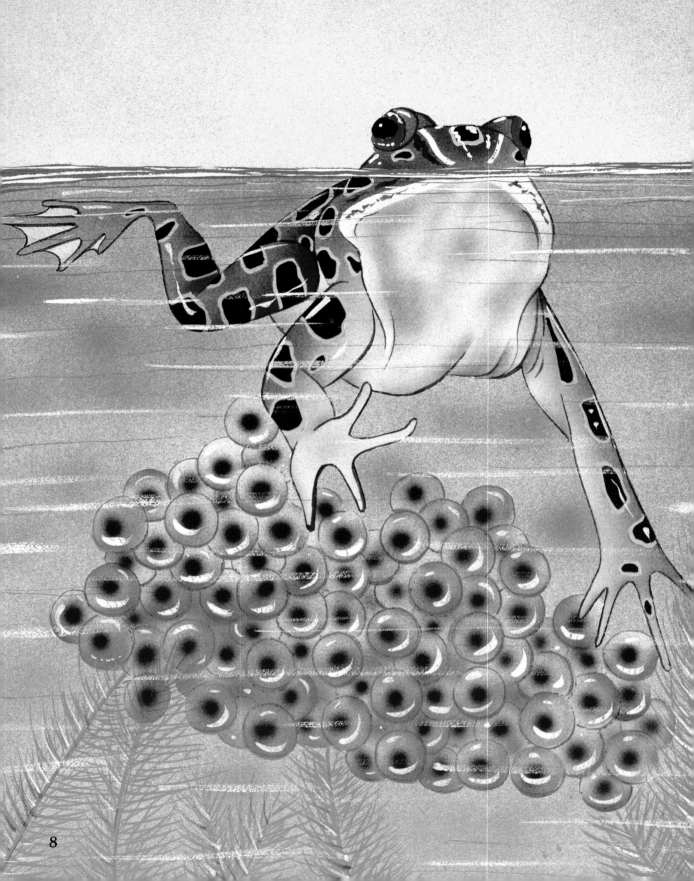

8

The frogs stay together, and swim around the pond. Soon the female lays many eggs. The male covers the eggs with sperm. Now the eggs can grow.

The two frogs swim away
leaving the eggs alone. Frog eggs
have no shell. In six days,
tadpoles hatch. They wiggle out of
the egg covering.

The new tadpole is very small.
At first it has no eyes or mouth. It
breathes with gills, the way a baby
fish does.

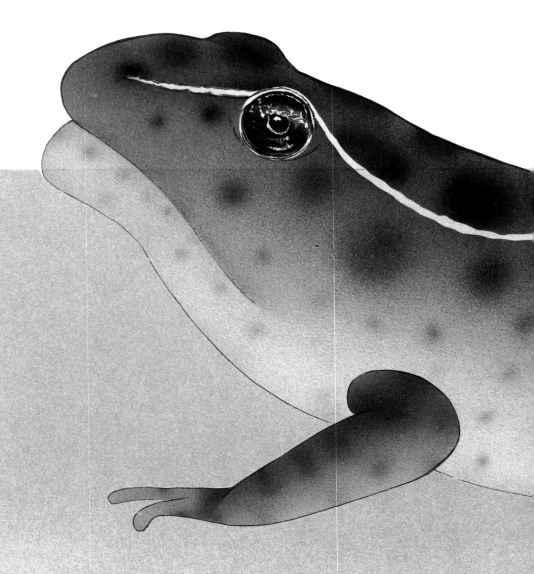

Every day the tadpole grows
larger. Now it has eyes and a
mouth and eats plants. The gills
are under its skin. The back legs
begin to grow. Its tail gets shorter
and shorter.

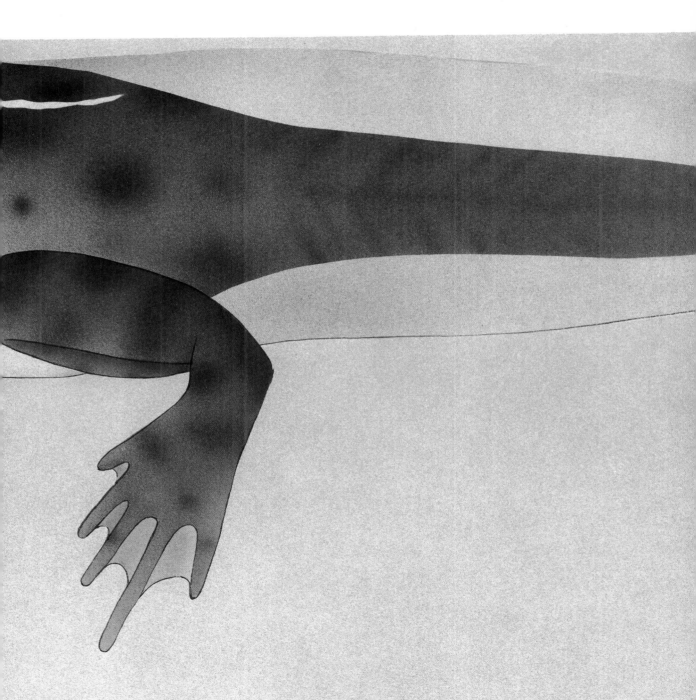

When the tail is almost gone, the tadpole becomes a frog. Now it breathes with lungs. With one hop, the frog goes a long way. It catches insects with its tongue.

In late summer, the young leopard frog leaves the pond. It goes to live in the tall grass. The frog stays where it is cool. The hot sun could kill it.

Most frogs never go far from water. When danger is near, they hop back to their pond. Many animals like to eat frogs.

Slippery skin makes the frog
hard to catch. Animals cannot
hold it easily. The frog drinks
through its skin.

When the weather turns cold, the frog gets ready for winter. It hops back to the pond. It digs a hole at the bottom.

All winter the frog sleeps
covered with mud. Air from the
water keeps it alive. It breathes
through its skin.

The spring sun warms the water. The frog wakes up. It wiggles out of the mud. A new year begins for the frog.

blue-legged strawberry frog

Frogs live around the world. The blue-legged strawberry frog lives in Costa Rica. Madagascar is the home of the golden mantella frog. The painted reed frog is from South Africa.

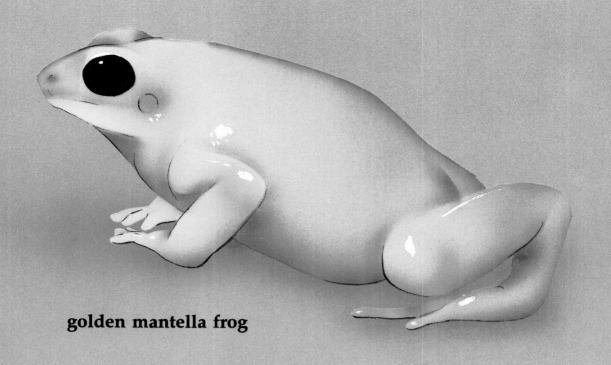

golden mantella frog

painted reed frog